D1199345

Where Words

Up and Down

by Tami Johnson

Capstone press

Mankato, Minnesota

A+ Books are published by Capstone Press,
151 Good Counsel Drive, P.O. Box 669, Mankato, Minnesota 56002.
www.capstonepress.com

1 2 3 4 5 6 12 11 10 09 08 07

Library of Congress Cataloging-in-Publication Data
Johnson, Tami.
   Up and down / by Tami Johnson.
   p. cm.—(A+ books. Where words)
   ISBN-13: 978-0-7368-6734-4 (hardcover)
   ISBN-10: 0-7368-6734-1 (hardcover)
   ISBN-13: 978-0-7368-7852-4 (softcover pbk.)
   ISBN-10: 0-7368-7852-1 (softcover pbk.)
   1. Orientation—Juvenile literature. I. Title.
BF299.O7J645 2007
153.7'52—dc22   2006022822

Summary: Simple text and color photographs introduce the basic concept of up and down.

Credits

Megan Schoeneberger, editor; Juliette Peters, designer; Charlene Deyle, photo researcher;
   Scott Thoms, photo editor

Photo Credits

Capstone Press/Karon Dubke, 6, 16–17; Capstone Press/Kyle Grenz, 29 (bottom); Corbis/Corbis/
Andrew Fox, 24; Corbis/D. Robert & Lorri Franz, 11; Corbis/Haruyoshi Yamaguchi, 23; Corbis/Mark
E. Gibson, 20; Corbis/Michele Westmorland, cover; Corbis/Niall Benvie, 10; Corbis/Patrik Giardino,
19; Corbis/Pete Saloutos, 18; Corbis/Randy Faris, 7; Corbis/Reuters/Alessandro Bianchi, 21; Corbis/
Reuters/Simon Kwong, 29 (top); Corbis/Steve Chenn, 8; Corbis/zefa/Birgid Allig, 26–27; Corbis/zefa/
Markus Botzek, 13; Gem Photo Studio/Tim Nehotte, 4–5; Getty Images Inc./Stone/Renee Lynn, 14;
Getty Images Inc./Taxi/Benelux Press, 15; Inspired Images, 28 (top); Minden Pictures/Tim Fitzharris,
12; PhotoEdit Inc./Spencer Grant, 9; Shutterstock/Cary Kalscheuer, 22; Shutterstock/Hway Kiong Lim,
25; Shutterstock/www.RestonImages.com, 28 (bottom)

Note to Parents, Teachers, and Librarians

Where Words uses color photographs and a nonfiction format to introduce readers to the vocabulary
of space. *Up and Down* is designed to be read aloud to a pre-reader, or to be read independently
by an early reader. Images and activities encourage mathematical thinking in early readers and
listeners. The book encourages further learning by including the following sections: Table of Contents,
Fun Facts, Glossary, Read More, Internet Sites, and Index. Early readers may need assistance using
these features.

Table of Contents

What Is Up? What Is Down?

Up is going higher.
Down is going lower.

At the playground, we climb up to slide down.

5

A balloon floats up.

A ball bounces down.

At school, we raise
our hands up when
we know the answer.

8

We sit down to listen
to a story.

Animals Up and Down

A squirrel climbs up the tree to its nest.

A squirrel scampers
down the tree to
find nuts buried
in the ground.

Ducks flap their wings
to fly up into the sky.

Ducks spread their wings
and glide down to the water.

An elephant raises its trunk up
to get leaves to eat from the tree.

An elephant lowers its trunk down
to the water for a drink.

People Up and Down

Boing! The girl jumps up
when the boy comes down.

17

A diver springs up
from the diving board.

A diver plunges
down to the pool.

19

Some people climb up
high to do their jobs.

Some people go down
low to do their jobs.

Roller coasters climb up slowly.

But the trip down is wild and fast.

Some birds work upside down
to build a nest.

Ducks dabble upside down
to find their food.

Everything looks different when we see things upside down.

Up and Down Facts

How deep down can a person dive in the ocean? British diver Mark Ellyat safely made a dive down more than 1,000 feet (305 meters) in water off the coast of Thailand. He made the dive down in just 12 minutes.

To get to the top of the Pyramid of Kukulcan in Mexico, visitors must walk up 91 steps. Each of the other three sides has exactly the same number of steps.

How do you go up to the top of the world's tallest building in Taipei, Taiwan? The elevator travels more than 30 miles (48 kilometers) per hour. Passengers can go from the fifth floor up to the 89th floor in less than 40 seconds.

How deep is the deepest hole ever drilled? You'll find it on the Kola Peninsula in Russia. Workers started drilling the hole in 1970 to study rocks deep inside Earth. By 1994 they had drilled down more than 40,000 feet (12,192 meters). That's more than 7 miles (11 kilometers) down.

Mount Everest
5.5 miles (8.9 kilometers) high

sea level

Kola Well
7 miles (11 kilometers) deep

Glossary

dabble (DAB-uhl)—to tilt the body forward and downward in water to get food

glide (GLIDE)—to move smoothly and easily

plunge (PLUHNJ)—to dive into water

pyramid (PIHR-uh-mid)—a solid shape with triangular sides that meet at a point on top

roller coaster (ROH-ler KOHSS-tur)—an amusement park ride with a train of cars that travel fast over a track that has rises, falls, and curves

scamper (SKAM-pur)—to run lightly and quickly

spread (SPRED)—to stretch out

spring (SPRING)—to jump suddenly

trunk (TRUHNGK)—the long nose of an elephant

upside down (UHP-side DOUN)—with the top at the bottom

Read More

Bailey, Jacqui. *Up, Down, All Around: A Story of Gravity.* Science Works. Minneapolis: Picture Window Books, 2006.

Gordon, Sharon. *Up/Down.* Bookworms. Just the Opposite. New York: Benchmark Books, 2004.

Murphy, Patricia J. *Up and Down.* Rookie Read-About Science. New York: Children's Press, 2002.

Internet Sites

FactHound offers a safe, fun way to find Internet sites related to this book. All of the sites on FactHound have been researched by our staff.

Here's how:

1. Visit *www.facthound.com*

2. Choose your grade level.

3. Type in this book ID **0736867341** for age-appropriate sites. You may also browse subjects by clicking on letters, or by clicking on pictures and words.

4. Click on the **Fetch It** button.

FactHound will fetch the best sites for you!

Index